Gerngross · Puchta · Becker
PLAYWAY 3

PUPIL'S BOOK

What's your name?

I'm Max

⭐ **1** **Watch the story.** 2 **Listen and read.**

⭐ **2** 3/4 **Listen. Sing the song.**

3 1 5 **Listen and speak.**

First day at school

(Comic strip)

- Hi, I'm Emma. What's your name?
- I'm Peter.
- How are you?
- I'm good, thanks.
- Good morning, children.
- Good morning, Mrs Wilson.
- Goodbye, children.
- Goodbye, Mrs Wilson.

4 **Now do a role play.**

⭐ **1** 🔘 7/8 **Listen. Sing the song. Then test your partner.**

- 🟠 orange
- 🟢 green
- 🔵 blue
- 🟡 yellow
- ⚪ grey
- 🔴 red
- 🩷 pink
- ⚪ white
- ⚫ black
- 🟤 brown

1, 2, 3, 4
5, 6, 7
8, 9, 10

Hello again

Hey, Hey

All right !

⭐ **2 Play a game in class.**

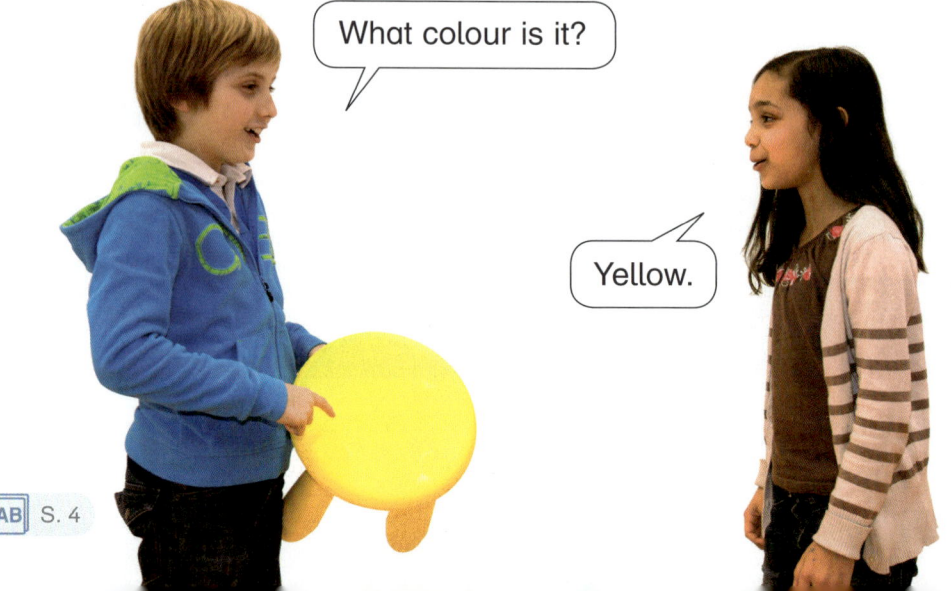

What colour is it?

Yellow.

★ **3** 🔘 ¹⁰ **Listen and point.**

★ **4** **Work in pairs.**

> What colour is the skateboard?

> It's pink and brown.

LOOK!

What colour **is** the bike?
It's blue. (**It's = It is**)

⭐ **5** 12-14 **Listen. Do the chant.**

Give me red

Give me red.
Here you are.

Give me yellow.
Here you are.

Give me green.
Here you are.

Give me blue.
Here you are.

Give me black.
Here you are.

Give me white.
Yeah, all right.

⭐ **6** **Work in pairs.**

The orange pencil, please.

Here you are.

 S. 6

Hello

★ **7** 📺 **Watch the story and say words you remember. Finish the sentences.**

1 Hello, I'm …

2 This is …

3 This is …

⭐ **8 Look and read. Then draw and speak.**

This is my friend, Philip.

This is my friend, Brownie.

★ **9** 🎵 16 **Listen and point. Then test your partner.**

1 one
2 two
3 three
4 four
5 five
6 six
7 seven
8 eight
9 nine
10 ten

★ **10** 🎵 17 **Listen and read.**

Phone numbers

⭐ **11** Make a chart. Hold interviews and make notes.

NAME	TELEPHONE NUMBER
Eva	9 8 3 6 5 4
Maria	3 2 4 …
Tom	7 5 8 …
Niki	3 1 0 …

⭐ **12** Use poster paper. Make a chart for your class.

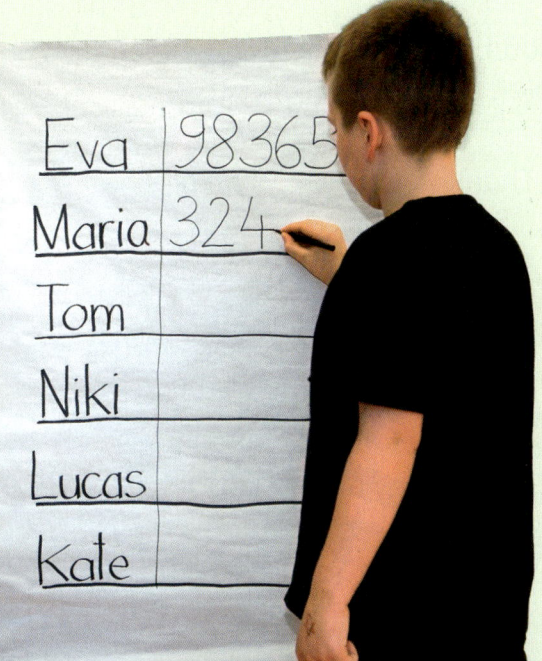

KV 3

★ **1** 🎧 19 **Listen and point. Then test your partner.**

1 pencil case
2 rubber
3 ruler
4 pencil
5 scissors
6 pen
7 book
8 glue stick
9 chair
10 schoolbag
11 desk

⭐ **2** **Work in pairs.**

Can I have the ruler, please?

Thank you.

Here you are.

⭐ 3 🎧 23-25 Listen. Do the chant.

scissors

pen

pencil case

book

pencil

Baby Face

Schoolbag, pencil, pencil case,
scissors, pen, book, Baby Face!
Sit down!

schoolbag

Baby Face

⭐ 4 Play the game.

In my schoolbag, there's a yellow ruler.

In my schoolbag, there's a yellow ruler and a red pen.

In my schoolbag, there's a yellow ruler, a red pen and a green book.

2 School

 5 26 **Listen and say.**

LOOK!

one glue stick – two glue stick**s**

one book – two book**s**

It's number …

 **6 Play the game.**

There are two glue sticks on the desk.

It's picture number 2.

LOOK!

There'**s** one pencil.
(There'**s** = There **is**)

There **are** three pencils.

⭐ 7 🎧 28 Listen and point.

⭐ 8 Say and mime.

Take a
pencil.

⭐ **9** **Read the text. Find the correct picture.**

On Lisa's desk, there are four pencils, a pen, three books and a glue stick.

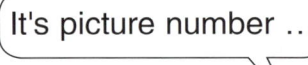
It's picture number …

⭐ **10** **Play a guessing game.**

On the desk, there are …

It's picture number …

My text ✏️

⭐ **11** **Read. Write your own text.**

My text
My schoolbag is cool.
It's red and green.

⭐ **12** **Read. Write your own text.**

My text
In my schoolbag, there's a blue pencil case and there are four books.
In my pencil case, there are two pencils, a pen, a ruler, a rubber and a glue stick.

A special guest

13 Look at the photos. Guess the answers. Watch the story and check.

- Who is Mia?
- Who is Mike?
- Who is the guest?
- Who is the teacher?

Number 1 is …

A group project: A guest in your class

Practise role plays in groups.

you / your friends	guest
Hello, I'm …	Hello, I'm …
How are you?	I'm good. / OK. / Great. And you?
This is …	Nice to meet you.
This is my class / school. There are … girls and … boys.	
Look. This is my pencil / schoolbag / …	Cool. / Very nice.
Mrs / Mr …, this is (Paula) …	Hello, Mrs / Mr …

you / your friends

guest

★ **1** 🎵 30 **Listen and point. Then test your partner.**

1 monkey
2 bat
3 elephant
4 fox
5 lion
6 bird
7 hippo
8 crocodile
9 frog
10 snake
11 rat

SAM'S SAFARI PARK

★ **2** **Play the game.**

What is it?

No, it isn't.

Yes, it is.

Is it the crocodile?

Is it the snake?

SNAKE

★ 3 🎵 31 **Listen and point. Test your partner.**

12   *15*   18   *11*   19
16   13   17   20   *14*

★ 4 Count the animals. Make notes on a piece of paper.

★ 5 Check with a partner.

How many snakes are there?

17

L👀K!

How many crocodile**s** are there?
How many fox**es** are there?

The lion is ill

 6 **Watch the story.** 🔘¹ 33 **Listen and read.**

★ **7** 34/35 **Listen. Sing the song.**

Listen to the animals

Listen to the elephant. *Doo doo doo!*
Listen to the hippo. *Doo doo doo!*
Listen to the monkey. *Doo doo doo doo!*
Listen to the snake. *Sssss!*

What a wonderful song, one, two, three,
come on, sing and dance with me!
What a wonderful song, one, two, three,
come on, sing and dance with me!

★ **8** **Work in groups. Sing the song using other animal words.**

Listen to the crocodile …

Animals

⭐ **9** 🔊 36 **Listen and point.**

⭐ **10** 🔊 37 **Listen and say the rhyme.**

Crocky, the crocodile

Hello, I'm Crocky, the crocodile.
I don't like elephants.
I don't like bats.
I like frogs
and I like rats.
Hehehehehe.

⭐ **11** **Make a list. Talk to your partner.**

My zoo

12 Read the text. Find the correct picture.

In my crazy zoo, there are
five elephants and eleven birds.
The elephants are red and blue.
The birds are orange and green.

It's picture number …

13 1 38 Listen to the rhyme. Then practise it.

This is my super zoo.
Come and see it – it's for you.

There are **fifteen** elephants,
there are **nineteen** frogs,
there are **thirteen** snakes,
but there are no dogs.

There are **eleven** crocodiles,
there are **fourteen** rats,
there are **twenty** hippos,
but there are no cats.

14 Write your own rhyme.

KV 9   **21**

⭐ **1** 🔘 39 **Listen and point. Then test your partner.**

1. woolly hat
2. pullover
3. jeans
4. trainers
5. T-shirt
6. mittens
7. boots
8. cap
9. jacket
10. skirt
11. tights
12. socks
13. shoes

⭐ **2** **Look at the picture and speak.**

Do you like the cap?

No, I don't.

Yes, I do.

Poster 4   AB S. 18

The T-shirt

⭐ **3** 📺 **Watch the story and say words you remember. Finish the sentences.**

Can I ...?

Can I ...?

Take ...!

... me!

 4 💿 43 **Listen and read.**

Shop assistant:	Good morning.
Noah + Vicky:	Good morning.
Noah:	A blue cap, please.
Shop assistant:	Here you are.
Noah:	I like it.
Vicky:	I don't like it. Take it off.
Noah:	OK.
Vicky:	This cap is nice. Put it on.
Noah:	Yeah. It's cool. I'll take it.

 **5 Do a role play.**

23

★ 6 🔘 44-46 Listen. Do the chant.

Cold and hot

It's cold outside.
Put on your jacket.
It's cold outside.
Put on your hat.
It's cold outside.
Put on your mittens.
OK, let's go.

Let's go inside.
OK, let's go.
It's hot in here.
Take off your mittens.
It's hot in here.
Take off your hat.
It's hot in here.
Take off your jacket.
Ah, that's better.

★ 7 Play the guessing game.

LOOK!

her cap   his cap

Finn

Toby

Anna

Lara

Charlie

Maria

Her cap is pink and her jeans are red.

No, her jacket is green.

It's Anna.

It's Maria.

The woolly hat

Father Bear has a hobby.
He makes woolly hats.

Joe, this hat is for you.

Oh, thank you!

Joe is not happy.

I hate it. Ahhrgh!

It's time for school.

Bye-bye, Joe.

Bye, Dad.

Bye-bye, woolly hat.

Oh, what a lovely hat.

Ah, it's Fred the fox.

Fred puts the hat on.

Ah, what a lovely hat. Wonderful!

Joe is in the classroom.

Stupid me.

⭐ **9** Read the text. Find the correct picture.

> Her woolly hat is yellow, her pullover is green, her skirt is red, her tights are blue and her trainers are white.

> It's picture number …

⭐ **10** Play a guessing game.

> Her woolly hat is …

> It's picture number …

My text ✏️

⭐ **11** Read. Write your own text.

My text

I like my blue and white jacket.
I don't like my black shoes.

⭐ **12** Read. Write your own text.

My text

Her cap is pink. There is a bat on it. Her T-shirt is white. There is a crocodile on it. Her jacket is blue. Her jeans are white, her socks are pink and her trainers are yellow.

Favourite clothes

13 Make a grid. In groups, ask and answer questions. Make notes.

	T-shirt 1	T-shirt 2	T-shirt 3	T-shirt 4
Sophia	🙂	🙂	🙂	🙁
David	🙂	🙁	🙁	🙁
Lisa	🙁	🙂	🙁	🙂
Sam	🙂	🙁	🙂	🙁

What about T-shirt number …?
Do you like it?

Yes, I do.

No, I don't.

14 Write a group report. Then talk about your group.

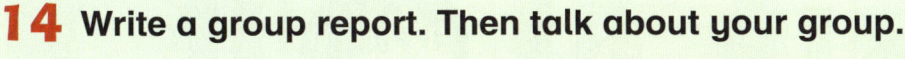

In our group, three kids like T-shirt number 1.

Two kids like T-shirt number 2.

Two kids like T-shirt number 3.

Only one kid likes T-shirt number 4.

1 brother

2 sister

3 mum

4 dad

5 aunt

6 uncle

7 grandma

8 grandpa

me

2 51 **Listen. Find Alisha's, Brandon's, Isabel's and Ryan's families.**

Family Photos

1

2

3

4

I think Alisha's family is number …

I think so too. /
I don't think so.
I think it's number …

AB S. 25 29

⭐ **3 Read and match.**

Hi, my name's Henry. We are three in our family. I've got a sister and there is my dad and me.

Hi, I'm Daniel. I've got a big family. There's my mum, my dad, my brother Mike, my grandpa, my grandma and me.

LOOK!
I've got – I have got

Hi, I'm Ella. I've got a sister. Her name's Holly. She is four years old. Then there's my mum, my grandma and me.

Hi, I'm Ann. In my family there's my mum, my dad and me.

I think Ann's family is number …

The raccoons and the beaver

★ **4** **Watch the story.** 52 **Listen and read.**

The raccoons are going for a picnic: Dad, Mum, Rosie and her brother, Ronnie.

Let's go to the river!

Yes, great!

OK.

What's that?

HELP!

It's a beaver over there.

HELP! HELP!

Let's help him.

Mum, Dad, Ronnie and his sister want to help. They swim across the river.

Pull! Pull!

HELP!

Go away.

Cut off his tail!

I've got an idea.

Just a minute.

HELP! HELP!

One, two, three ... jump.

It works.

Now let's have our picnic.

Yes, great!

The beaver is very happy. Mum, Dad, Rosie and her brother, Ronnie, are happy too.

Mmmh. That's good. Yummy.

 5 53/54 **Listen. Sing the song.**

The clever raccoons

The clever raccoons are helpful.
The clever raccoons are strong.
Ronnie and Rosie, Dad and Mum.
The clever raccoons, oh, here they come!

A bushy tail and two small ears,
a funny face and a black nose.
That's Rosie, the clever raccoon.

A bushy tail and two small ears,
a funny face and a black nose.
That's Ronnie, he's Rosie's brother.

My text ✏

 6 Read. Write your own text.

My text

My mum, my two sisters and me.
This is my family.

 7 Read. Write your own text.

My text

My name is Tom. I'm 8 years old. I've got a brother and a sister.
His name is David and her name is Barbara.

Mia & Mike

Families

 8 Look at the photos. Guess the answers. 📺 Then watch the video and check.

1

2

3

4

Who is …
- Mia's mum?
- Mia's dad?
- Mia's sister?
- Mike's mum?
- Mike's brother?
- Mike's sister?

Number 1 is …

5

6

A project: Present your family

Bring photos or draw pictures of your family. Present your family.

This is my mum / dad.
This is my sister / brother (Jenny / Bob).
He's / She's … (years old).
This is my …

Presentation tip:
✔ Loud and clear!
✔ Smile.
✔ Point at your picture / photo.

★ **1** 🎧 1 **Listen and point. Then test your partner.**

1. hand
2. arm
3. shoulder
4. head
5. ear
6. hair
7. eye
8. nose
9. mouth
10. tooth / (four) teeth
11. finger
12. knee
13. toe
14. leg
15. foot / (two) feet

★ **2** **Play the game. Throw the ball and say body words.**

★ **3**  2-4 **Listen. Do the chant.**

Bend your knees

Bend your knees.

Touch your toes.

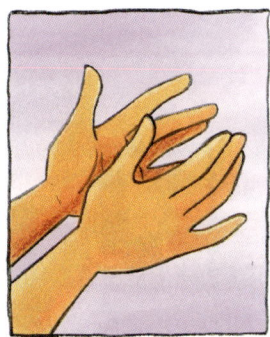

Clap your hands.

Touch your nose.

Shake your fingers.

Touch your hair.

Stamp your feet.

Touch your chair.

Shake your head.

Jump up high.

Grow and grow.

Touch the sky.

★ **4** **Play the game.**

Simon says,
'Clap your hands'.

Mr Matt keeps fit

★ **5** 📺 Watch the story and say words you remember. Finish the sentences.

1 Now touch …

2 … idea!

3 Give …!

4 Come …

✨ **6** Do a role play.

Shake your fingers.
Bend your knees.
One, two, three.
Now jump!
Come on, lazy!

★ **7** 🎵 7/8 **Listen. Sing the song.**

The body rock

Let's rock, the rock, the body rock, yeah!
Listen everybody,
get ready for the rock,
the rock, the rock, the body rock, yeah!

Shake your body to the beat,
arms and hands and legs and feet,
head and hair and ears and nose,
come on, shake, from head to toes.

Boys and girls, join in, please,
touch your toes and touch your knees,
touch your ears, your nose, your lips,
clap your hands and touch your hips.

★ **8** **Point and test your partner.**

Shake your body.

🕐 KV 16   **37**

★ 9 9 **Listen and read. Match the dialogues with the correct picture.**

Dialogue 1:

A: Ouch!

B: What's the problem?

A: My tummy hurts.

B: Have a cup of tea.

A: OK.

Dialogue 2:

C: Ouch!

D: What's the matter?

C: My left knee hurts.

D: Let me see.

C: Ouch! Don't touch it!

D: Sorry! Let's go to the doctor's.

C: OK, Dad.

Dialogue 1 is picture number …

★ 10 Make dialogues.

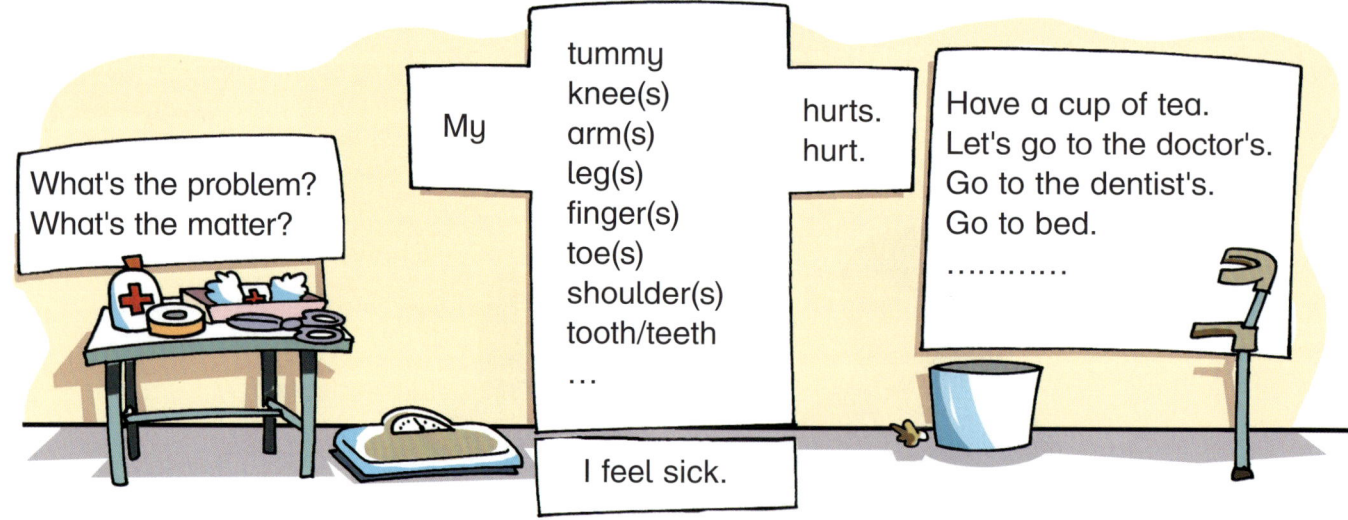

What's the problem?
What's the matter?

My — tummy / knee(s) / arm(s) / leg(s) / finger(s) / toe(s) / shoulder(s) / tooth/teeth / … — hurts. hurt.

Have a cup of tea.
Let's go to the doctor's.
Go to the dentist's.
Go to bed.
…………

I feel sick.

Monsters

⭐ **11 Read, look and say.**

> His hair is black, his nose is red and his teeth are yellow.

①

②

> It's picture number …

⭐⭐ **12** 🔘 11 **Listen to the poem and practise it.**

His eyes are red.
His hair is pink.
His teeth are black.
He's got five legs
and four green arms.

Let's play a game.
What's his name?

⭐⭐ **13 Write your own poem and draw a picture.**

⭐ **1** 🎧 13 **Listen and point. Then test your partner.**

1 rain
It's raining.

2 snow
It's snowing.

3 cloud
It's cloudy.

4 fog
It's foggy.

5 wind
It's windy.

6 sun
It's sunny.

⭐ **2** 🎧 14-16 **Listen. Do the chant.**

A cap on a cat

A cap on a cat.
A cap on a dog.
A cap on a rabbit.
A cap on a frog.
Rain, snow or sun,
caps are always fun.

The little seed

⭐ **3** 📺 **Watch the story.** 🎵 17 **Listen and read.**

★ **4** 🎧 18 **Listen. What are the animals' names? Say the rhyme.**

Scott	Jane	Peter	Stuart	Joe

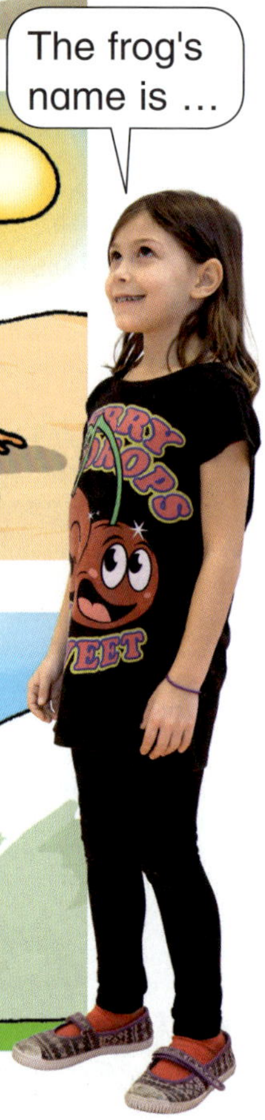

> The frog's name is …

★ **5** 🎧 19 **Listen and point.**

spring	summer	autumn	winter

6 Read. Answer the questions.

- Which photo shows a rainbow?
- Which photo shows a hurricane?
- Which photo shows a farm?

Hi, I'm Amy and I live in Florida.
The weather here is fantastic. There is one problem: sometimes we get hurricanes.
Hurricanes are very strong winds.
Can you find my photo?

Hi, I'm John.
I live in Ireland. It rains a lot here. It rains in winter, in spring, in summer and in autumn. It's always green here.
Can you find my photo?

Hello, I'm Judy.
I live on a farm in Australia. In summer it is very hot. Sometimes it rains in winter.
Can you find my photo?

Hello, I'm Mike and I live in Canada.
There is a lot of snow in winter and it is very cold.
Can you find my photo?

7 Work in pairs and say *True* or *False*.

1. It never rains in Ireland.
2. John is from Australia.
3. Amy is from Florida.
4. There's a lot of snow in Australia.
5. Judy lives on a farm.
6. It rains a lot in Florida.

★ **8** 🎵 22/23 **Listen. Sing the song.**

Crazy weather

On Monday, it's cloudy,
on Tuesday, there's rain.
On Wednesday, there's sun,
and on Thursday, rain again!

On Friday, it's foggy,
it's cloudy and cold;
but on Saturday and Sunday,
there's sun – it looks like gold!

Oh, yeah, the weather's crazy,
it's crazy, yeah, that's true!
Sun, rain, fog or snow?
You never, never know!

 9 **Play the guessing game.**

	Monday	Tuesday	Wednesday	Thursday	Friday	Saturday	Sunday
London	sunny	cloudy	foggy	rainy	rainy	windy	sunny
New York	rainy	cloudy	foggy	rainy	rainy/sunny	sunny	sunny
Sydney	cloudy	windy	sunny	sunny	sunny	cloudy	rainy
Toronto	windy	sunny/cloudy	sunny	sunny	cloudy	foggy	rainy

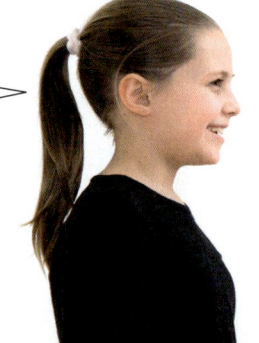

On Tuesday it's cloudy.
On Thursday it's raining.
On Friday it's raining
and sunny.

It's New York.

KV 20

Weather and seasons

⭐⭐ **10** Make a weather chart on a piece of paper. Make notes.

	MONDAY	TUESDAY	WEDNESDAY	THURSDAY	FRIDAY	SATURDAY	SUNDAY
MORNING	SUNNY	FOGGY	RAINING	SUNNY	RAINING		
AFTERNOON	CLOUDY	CLOUDY	CLOUDY				

A week later: Ask your partner.

What was your favourite day last week?
What was the weather like?

My favourite day was Thursday.
It was sunny.

⭐ **11** Make a grid. In groups, ask and answer questions. Make notes.

Spring	Summer	Autumn	Winter
Emma Sophie	Leo Paul Zoe		Philip

What's your favourite season?

⭐⭐ **12** Write a group report. Then talk about your group.

In our group, two kids like spring.
Three kids like …

⭐ **1** 🎧 24 **Listen and point. Then test your partner.**

1 pear
2 yoghurt
3 rice
4 chicken
5 apple
6 chips
7 fish
8 tomato soup
9 muesli bar
10 cheese sandwich
11 orange
12 broccoli
13 carrots
14 egg
15 peas
16 potatoes

⭐ **2** **Play the card game.**

Can I have the carrots?

Here you are.

3 25-27 **Listen. Do the chant.**

Lots of spaghetti

Lots of spaghetti
on a big, big plate.

With butter and cheese,
spaghetti is great.

Lots of chicken
on a big, big plate.

With ketchup and chips,
chicken is great.

4 Look and read. Say.

Lucy   **Dylan**   **Robert**   **Ella**

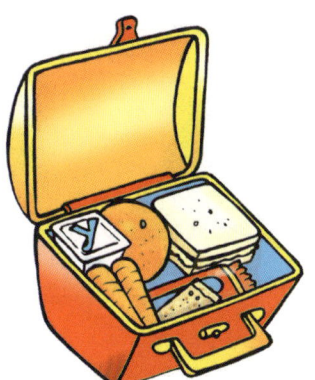

1 There's a yoghurt, there are two carrots, an orange, a muesli bar and a cheese sandwich.

2 There's an egg, there are two carrots, an orange, a muesli bar and a cheese sandwich.

3 There's an egg, there are two carrots, an orange, a muesli bar and two cheese sandwiches.

4 There's a yoghurt, there are two apples, an orange, a muesli bar and a cheese sandwich.

LOOK!

a muesli bar
an orange

Lucy's lunch box is number …

KV 21   AB S. 39   **47**

What's for breakfast?

⭐ **5** Watch the story and say words you remember. Finish the sentences.

1

What's for …?

Just a minute.

2

… , no toast.

But, Dad! We're hungry!

3

Hey, …

4

… , there are two more eggs.

⭐ **6** 28 Listen and read.

Rob: Good morning.

Dad: Good morning.

Rob: I'm hungry. What's for breakfast?

Dad: Egg on toast?

Rob: Great.

Dad: And to drink?

Rob: Can I have some tea?

Dad: Yes, of course.

⭐ **7** Do a role play.

⭐ **8** **Read the text. Find the correct picture.**

> I like tomatoes. My favourite lunch is tomato soup.

> It's picture number …

⭐ **9** **Play a guessing game.**

> I like …

> It's picture number …

My text ✏️

⭐ **10** **Read. Write your own text.**

My text

I like chicken.

My favourite lunch is chicken

and rice. I don't like fish.

⭐ **11** **Read. Write your own text.**

My text

I like fish. My favourite lunch is fish and potatoes.

My number 2 favourite lunch is chicken with rice. I don't like broccoli.

In my favourite lunch box, there are two oranges, two muesli bars,

a cheese sandwich and an egg.

★ **12** 🔊 31 **Listen and point. Then test your partner.**

1. milk
2. orange juice
3. mineral water
4. hot chocolate
5. tea

✦ **13 Look and say.** 🔊 32 **Then listen and check.**

| orange juice | milk | hot chocolate | mineral water |

Helen

Harry

Isabel

Adam

Helen would like some …

What's for lunch?

⭐ **14** Look at the photos. Guess the answers. Then watch the video and check.

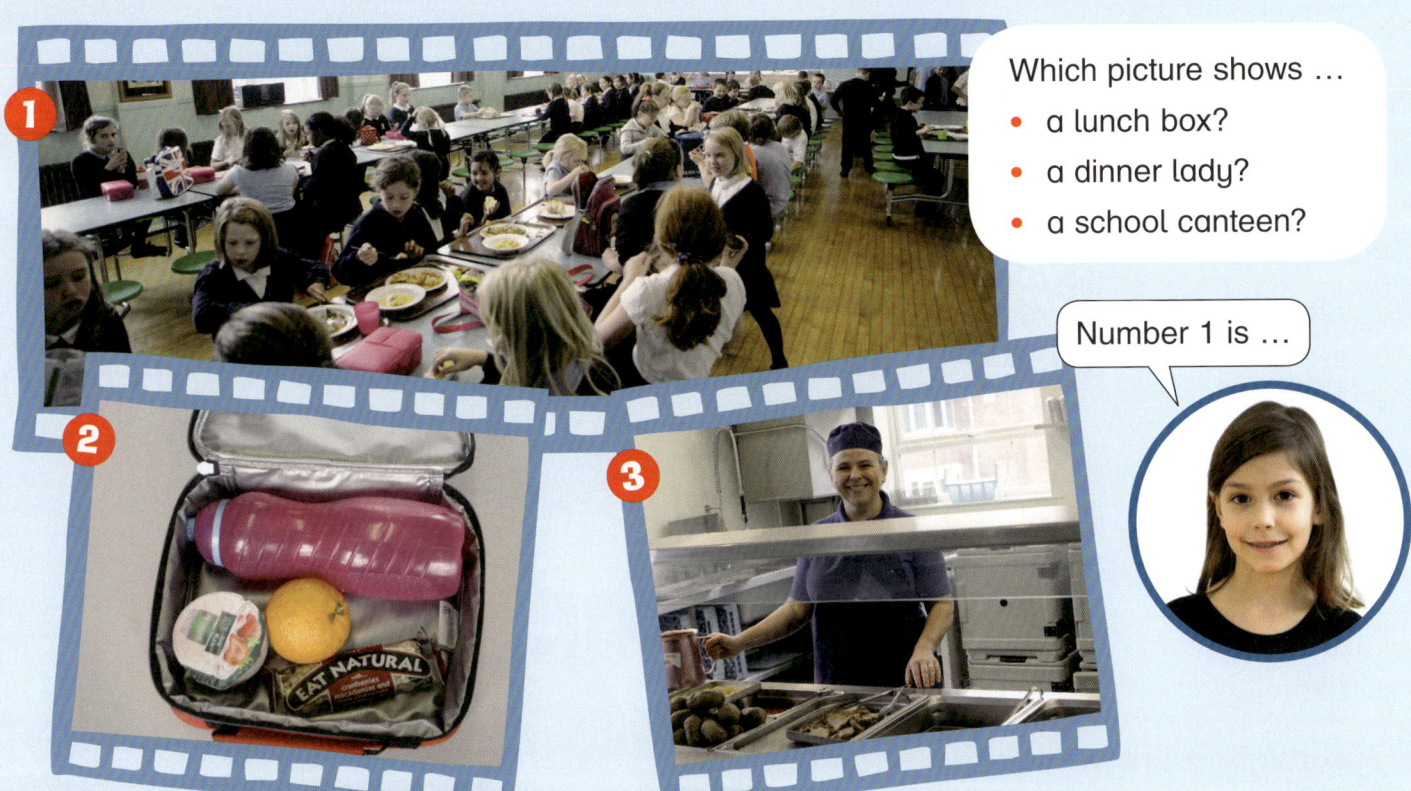

> Which picture shows …
> - a lunch box?
> - a dinner lady?
> - a school canteen?

> Number 1 is …

A group project: What's for lunch?

Make drawings of food. Cut them out and make a lunch box.

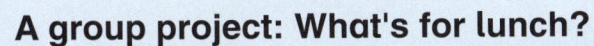

Put in five things for your partner and give it to him / her.

> Here's your lunch box.

> Thank you. Ah, I've got …

⭐ **1** 🎧 33 **Listen and point. Then test your partner.**

1 horse
2 cow
3 pig
4 hen
5 sheep
6 dog
7 rabbit
8 cat
9 duck
10 bee
11 earthworm

WELCOME TO HONEYBEE FARM

⭐ **2 Talk in class.**

I like pigs.

I don't like pigs. I like rabbits.

Yes, rabbits are nice.

★ 3 Look and answer.

Which picture shows …
- three big sheep?
- a big and a small dog?
- a big and a small cat?
- two small cows?
- three small hens?
- a big and a small horse?

LOOK!

a small dog   a big dog

1

2

★ 4 Look at the pictures. Say what is different.

LOOK!

There is one sheep.
There are three sheep.

In picture 1, there is one big hen and two small hens.

In picture 2, there are three small hens.

KV 24   AB S. 44   **53**

Eddie, the earthworm

★ **5** 📺 **Watch the story.** 🎧 34 **Listen and read.**

It's a lovely morning on the farm. This is Eddie, the earthworm.

Hi, everybody!

Who are you?

Hi, I'm Eddie, the earthworm.

I give milk. What about you?

I live underground.

Underground? Stupid!

Eddie is sad.

Who are you?

Hi, I'm Eddie, the earthworm.

I lay eggs. What about you?

I live underground.

Underground? Stupid!

Eddie is very sad.

Who are you?

Hi, I'm Eddie, the earthworm.

I make honey. What about you?

I live underground.

Underground? Stupid!

Eddie is very, very sad.

Hello, Eddie. You look sad. What's the problem?

I can't give milk, I can't lay eggs, and I can't make honey.

Eddie, you're the king of the garden.

Really?

Eddie, Eddie is the king of the garden. Eddie, Eddie, everybody loves you.

Yes, the flowers, the vegetables and the trees love you.

Oh, thank you very much.

Eddie is happy again.

AB S. 45

9

⭐ **6**   35/36 **Listen. Sing the song.**

The earthworm song

Hens lay eggs,
cows give milk,
and bees make honey.
Lots of eggs,
lots of milk,
and lots of honey.

But Eddie, Eddie
is the king of the garden.
Eddie, Eddie,
everybody loves you.

... but Eddie is the king!
Oh, yes!

⭐ **7** **Work in pairs. How many correct sentences can you make?**

Hens	can fly.
Earthworms	can swim.
Dogs	can't fly.
Cats	can't swim.
Cows	lay eggs.
Bees	give milk.
	make honey.
	can't climb trees.
	eat grass.
	can climb trees.

55

★ **8** 39 **Listen. Guess the animals.**

★ **9 Read the text. Find the correct picture.**

The animal can't fly.
It lays eggs. It can swim.

1 **2** **3**

✪ **10 Work in pairs. Make a riddle for your partner.**

It can fly. It makes honey. It can't swim. What is it?

It's a …

WORD PLAY

What my animal can do

⭐ **11** 💿2 40 **Listen and point. Test your partner.**

✴ **12** 💿2 41 **Listen to the poem and practise it.**

Oliver

Oliver, the sheep, can sing.
Oliver can jump up high.
Oliver can eat spaghetti.
But Oliver can't fly.

✴ **13** **Write your own poem and draw a picture.**

⭐ **1** 42/43 **Listen. Sing the song.**

Merry Christmas!

We wish you a Merry Christmas,
we wish you a Merry Christmas,
we wish you a Merry Christmas
and a Happy New Year!

⭐ **2** 44 **Listen and read.**

Hi, I'm Christina from Cambridge. This is our Christmas.

December 24: Christmas Eve
We hang up our Christmas stockings for the small presents. We put biscuits and a glass of milk for Father Christmas on a table.

December 25: Christmas Day
We open our presents in the morning.

Later we have Christmas dinner. We eat turkey, Christmas pudding and mince pies. Here you can see my brother Pete, my grandma and grandpa, and my mum and dad.

We pull open Christmas crackers. In each cracker, there's a paper hat, a joke and small presents.

Father Christmas is lost

⭐ **3** **Watch the story.** 45 **Listen and read.**

It's Christmas Day.

Sorry, we don't know.

There are no presents! Mum, Dad! Where are our presents?

Excuse me, I'm lost. Where's the farm?

Sorry, I'm in a hurry. Bye.

Brrrr! I'm cold. And I'm lost.

Excuse me. Excuse me, I'm lost. Where is the farm?

I'm sorry. I'm busy.

Oh, dear, oh, dear!

Excuse me, I'm lost. Where's the farm, please?

The farm? I'm sorry. I don't know.

Brrrr! I'm so cold!

Excuse me, I'm lost. Where's the farm, please?

Sorry?

The farm? Where's the farm?

It's over there.

Thanks very much.

You're welcome, Father Christmas.

Who is it?

It's Father Christmas!

Father Christmas! Welcome!

Sorry I'm late.

We wish you a Merry Christmas, ... and a Happy New Year!

★ **1** ⊙ 46 **Listen and read.**

The fourth Thursday in November is Thanksgiving Day in the USA.
People say thank you for the harvest.
On Thanksgiving Day, families eat turkey,
sweet potatoes and pumpkin pie.

★ **2 Look at the cartoon.**

The beginning of Thanksgiving

1620 in America:

The first winter:

I'm cold.

I'm hungry!

The first spring:

The first Thanksgiving (autumn 1621):

Thank you!

1 47/48 **Listen. Sing the song.**

Easter bunny

Easter bunny, come along.
Hush, hush, hop, hop, come along,
Easter bunny, come along,
hush, it's time to come along.

It's time for Easter eggs,
yellow, red and blue.
It's time for Easter eggs,
it's time for you.

2 49 **Listen and read.**

Before Easter, children make Easter cards at school. On Easter Sunday, many families have hot cross buns and boiled eggs for breakfast. For lunch, they have a big family meal. The children get big Easter eggs on Easter Sunday.

The bilby is a small Australian animal. It is in danger. Cats eat bilbies and rabbits eat their food. To help the bilby, Australians make chocolate Easter bilbies. 50 cents go to 'Save the bilby'.

 3 **Make a poster about your Easter. Speak.**

A

afternoon	Nachmittag
I **am**	ich **bin**
animal	Tier
apple	Apfel
you **are**; we **are**	du **bist**/ihr **seid**; wir **sind**
arm	Arm
She's **asleep.**	Sie **schläft.**
aunt	Tante
autumn	Herbst

B

bat	Fledermaus
beautiful	schön
beaver	Biber
bed	Bett
bee	Biene
bend	beugen
big	groß
bike	Fahrrad
bird	Vogel
biscuits	Kekse
black	schwarz
Bless you!	Gesundheit!
blue	blau
body	Körper
book	Buch
boots	Stiefel
boy	Junge
breakfast	Frühstück
broccoli	Brokkoli
brother	Bruder
brown	braun
bus stop	Bushaltestelle
butter	Butter
butterfly	Schmetterling
Bye-bye! / Bye!	Tschüss!

C

can/can't	können/nicht können
canteen	(Schul-)Kantine
cap	Mütze/Kappe
car	Auto
carrots	Karotten
cat	Katze
chair	Stuhl
cheese (sandwich)	**Käse**(sandwich)
chicken	Hähnchen
chips	Pommes frites
Merry **Christmas!**	Frohe **Weihnachten!**
clap	klatschen
classroom	Klassenzimmer
climb	klettern
close	schließen

clothes	Kleidung
cloud	Wolke
It's **cloudy.**	Es ist **wolkig.**
cold	kalt
colour	Farbe; anmalen
come	kommen
cow	Kuh
crazy	verrückt, lustig
crocodile	Krokodil
cut	schneiden

D

dad	Vater
dance	tanzen
dentist	Zahnarzt/-ärztin
desk	Tisch
dinner lady	Mitarbeiterin in der Schulkantine
do	tun, machen
dog	Hund
draw	zeichnen
drink	trinken; Getränk
duck	Ente

E

ear	Ohr
earthworm	Regenwurm
Easter (bunny)	**Ostern** (Osterhase)
eat	essen
lay **eggs**	**Eier** legen
elephant	Elefant
eye	Auge

F

face	Gesicht
false	falsch
family	Familie
fantastic	fantastisch
Father Christmas	Weihnachtsmann
favourite (drink)	**Lieblings…** (getränk)
fish	Fisch
flowers	Blumen
fly	fliegen
fog	Nebel
It's **foggy.**	Es ist **neblig.**
food	Speise
foot/feet	Fuß/Füße
fox	Fuchs
Friday	Freitag
friend	Freund/Freundin
frog	Frosch

G

garden	Garten
get up	aufstehen
girl	Mädchen
give	geben
glue stick	Klebestift
go	gehen
good	gut
Good morning.	Guten Morgen.
Goodbye.	Auf Wiedersehen.
grandma	Großmutter
grandpa	Großvater
grass	Gras
great	großartig
green	grün
grey	grau
grow	wachsen
guest	Gast

H

hair	Haar(e)
happy	glücklich
hat	Hut
hate	hassen
have	haben
head	Kopf
hear	hören
hello	hallo
help	helfen
hen	Henne
Here you are.	(Hier), bitte sehr. / Da hast du es.
hippo	Flusspferd
honey	Honig
horse	Pferd
hot	heiß
hot chocolate	heiße Schokolade
house	Haus
How are you?	Wie geht es dir/Ihnen?
How many ...?	Wie viele...?
hungry	hungrig
hurricane	Hurrikan/Wirbelsturm
My arm **hurts**.	Mein Arm **tut weh**.

I

idea	Idee
ill	krank
in	im, in
It **is** ...	Es **ist**...

J

jacket	Jacke
jump	springen

K

king	König
knee	Knie
knife	Messer

L

lay	legen
left	links
leg	Bein
like/don't like	mögen/nicht mögen
lion	Löwe
listen	zuhören
live	leben
look	schauen
lots of	viele
love	lieben
lunch	Mittagessen
lunch box	Pausenbrotdose

M

make	machen/anfertigen
me	mir/mich
(glass of) **milk**	(Glas) **Milch**
mineral water	Mineralwasser
mittens	Fäustlinge
Monday	Montag
monkey	Affe
mouth	Mund
muesli bar	Müsliriegel
mum	Mutter/Mama

N

nose	Nase
number	Nummer

O

open	öffnen
orange juice	Orangensaft
owl	Eule

P

pear	Birne
peas	Erbsen
pen	Stift, Füller
pencil	Bleistift
pencil case	Federmappe
pig	Schwein
plate	Teller
play	spielen
please	bitte
point	zeigen (auf)
potato/es	Kartoffel/n
presents	Geschenke
put on	anziehen

R

rabbit	Hase 
raccoon	Waschbär
rain	Regen
It's **raining**.	Es **regnet**.
rainbow	Regenbogen
rat 	Ratte
read	lesen
red	rot
rice	Reis
right	rechts
river	Fluss 
rubber	Radiergummi
ruler	Lineal 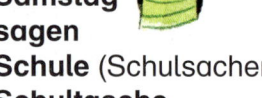

S

sad	traurig
Saturday	Samstag
say	sagen
school (things)	Schule (Schulsachen)
schoolbag	Schultasche
scissors	Schere
seasons	Jahreszeiten
seed	Samen; Keim
shake	schütteln
sheep 	Schaf/Schafe
shoes	Schuhe
shoulder	Schulter
I feel **sick**.	Mir ist **übel**.
sing	singen
sister	Schwester
sit (down)	(hin) **setzen**
skirt	Rock
sleep	schlafen
small	klein
smell	riechen
snake 	Schlange
snow	Schnee
It's **snowing**.	Es **schneit**.
socks	Socken
sorry	Entschuldigung.
speak	sprechen
spring	Frühling
stamp	stampfen
stand up	aufstehen
stockings	Strümpfe
strong	stark
summer	Sommer
sun	Sonne
It's **sunny**.	Es ist **sonnig**.
Sunday	Sonntag
sweet	süß
swim	schwimmen

T

tail	Schwanz
take	nehmen
take off	ausziehen
(a cup of) **tea**	(Tasse) **Tee** 
teacher	Lehrer/in
telephone number	Telefonnummer
Thanks. / Thank you.	Danke.
Thanksgiving	Erntedankfest
Thursday	Donnerstag
tick	anhaken; ankreuzen
tights	Strumpfhosen
toe(s)	Zeh(en)
tomato soup	Tomatensuppe
tooth/teeth	Zahn/Zähne
touch	berühren
trainers	Turnschuhe
tree	Baum
true	richtig
try on	anprobieren
Tuesday	Dienstag
tummy	Bauch

U

umbrella	Regenschirm
uncle	Onkel
underground	hier: **unter der Erde**

V

vegetables	Gemüse
very	sehr

W

wake up	aufwachen
want	wollen
watch	hier: **schauen**
we	wir
wear	anhaben/tragen
weather	Wetter
Wednesday	Mittwoch
What's the matter?	Was ist los?
What's your name?	Wie heißt du?
white	weiß
who	wer
It's **windy**.	Es ist **windig**. 
woodpecker	Specht
woolly hat	Wollmütze
write	schreiben

Y

year	Jahr
yellow	gelb
yoghurt	Jogurt
you	du/dich